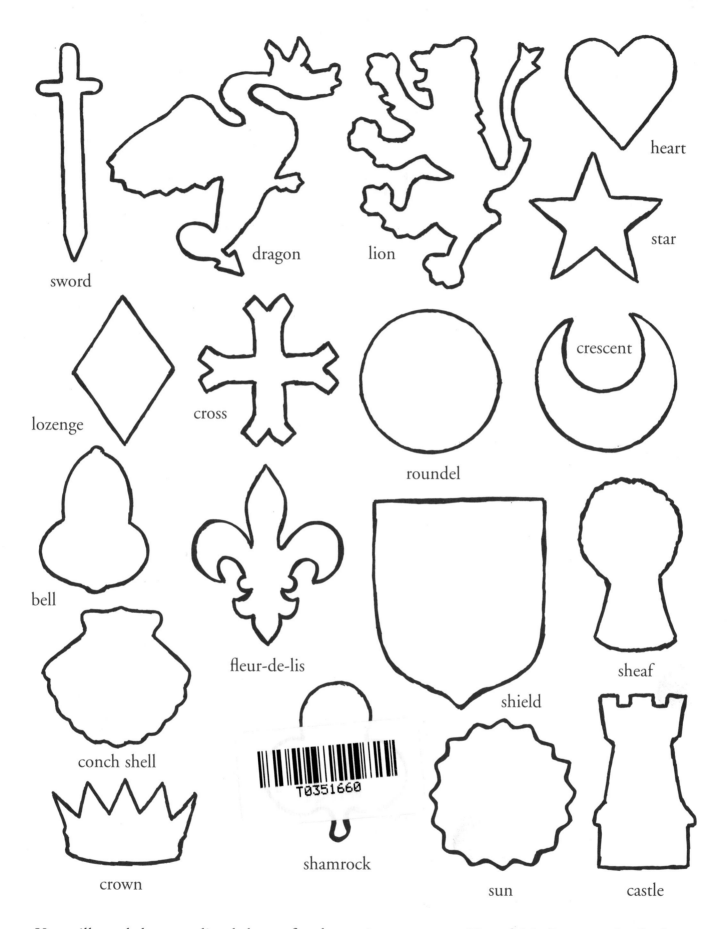

sword

dragon

lion

heart

star

lozenge

cross

roundel

crescent

bell

fleur-de-lis

shield

sheaf

conch shell

shamrock

sun

castle

crown

You will need these medieval shapes for the projects on pages 20 and 22. See opposite for how to use them. These instructions replace the ones on page 24.

T0351660

i

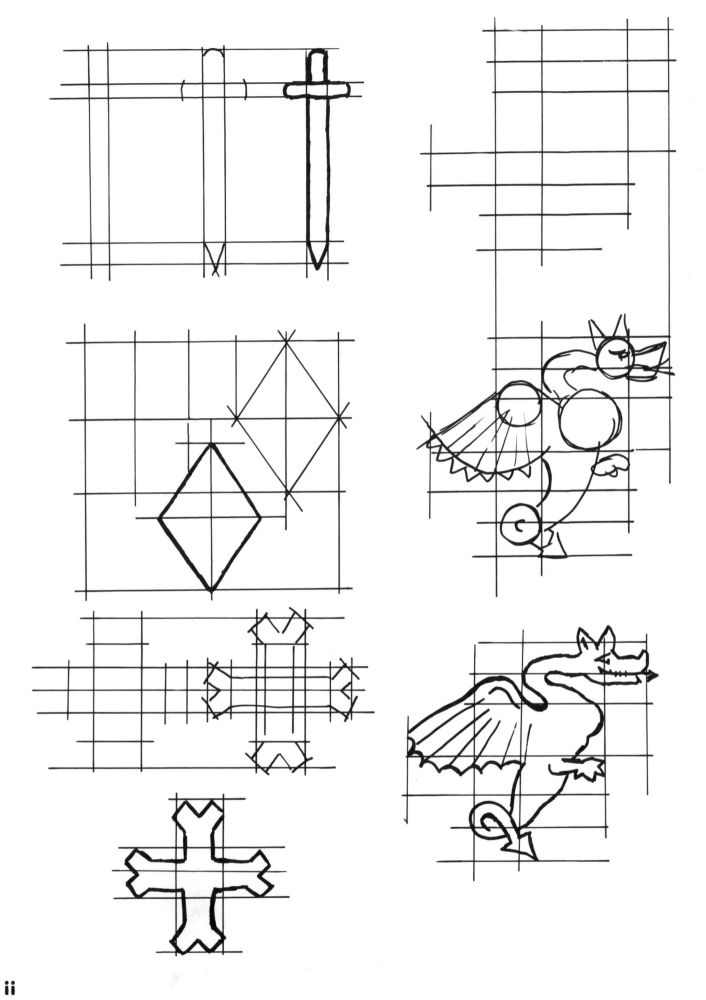

CONTENTS

Whatever you choose to make first you'll need plenty of packaging, so it's a good idea to start collecting it in advance. Ask people to save things for you instead of throwing them away.

You can flatten cardboard boxes and cereal packets to save space. Rinse plastic bottles and leave them to dry. Prepare an area to work in and have lots of old newspapers handy if you are using glue and paints.

HOW TO MAKE A CROWN

Kings and queens were very powerful people in the Middle Ages. They were always plotting and fighting over who should wear the crown, so here is one for each of them.

YOU'LL NEED:
2 pieces of paper 62 x 10 cm, thin card, scissors, ruler, pencil, tracing paper, masking tape, glue, paints and/or metallic pens.

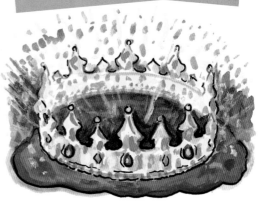

62 cm

10 cm

2-cm tab

1 Draw six pencil lines on the paper 10 cm apart.

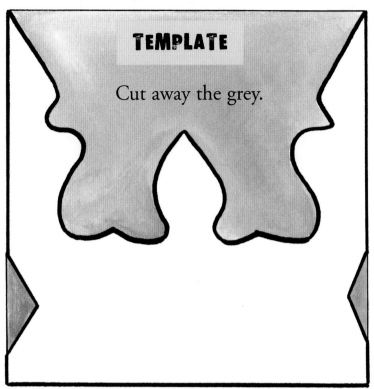

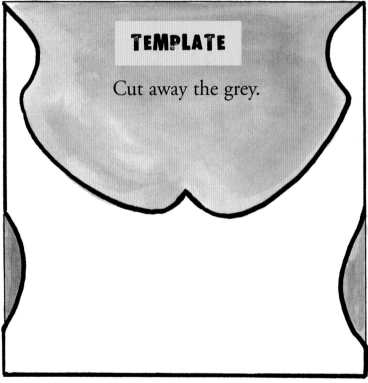

TEMPLATE

Cut away the grey.

TEMPLATE

Cut away the grey.

⭐ **2** Fold the paper along these lines.

⭐ **3** Copy the templates on to the card (using the instructions on the inside front cover). Cut them out.

⭐ **4** Use them to draw the crown outlines on to the paper.

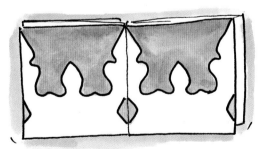

⭐ **5** Cut out the outlines as shown. If the paper is too thick to cut, open it out and draw two outlines to cut round.

⭐ **6** Fit to your head and glue the ends together. Decorate with paints and/or pens.

3

HOW TO BUILD YOUR OWN FOLD-UP CASTLE

Now you have a crown, you need a castle to protect it. Thousands of castles were built all across Europe during the Middle Ages. Every ruler wanted theirs to be the biggest and the best with all the latest defences. Prague Castle in the Czech Republic and Windsor Castle in England are two of the biggest still in one piece.

YOU'LL NEED:
Large cardboard packing box (from a chair or fridge), Velcro self-adhesive tape, PVA glue, craft knife, scissors, ruler, marker pen, paints and brushes.

TOP TIP – TOP TIP
Cut some slits in the walls to keep a look-out for approaching enemy armies.

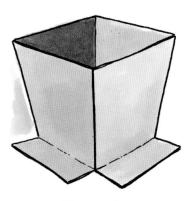

 1 Cut off the flaps except for two adjoining flaps at the bottom of the box. (Keep the cut-offs.)

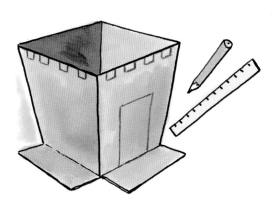

2 Mark out battlements and a drawbridge (on a side with a flap).

 3 Carefully cut them out, leaving the bottom of the drawbridge to form a hinge. Fold the bottom flaps under the box.

4 Glue a cut-off flap inside the top of the opening. Glue another to the inside of the drawbridge door so you can pull it shut.

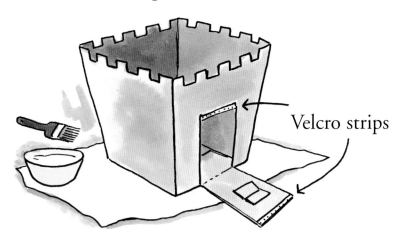

Velcro strips

5 Paint the whole box with PVA diluted with three times the amount of water and allow it to dry. Stick Velcro where shown.

6 Paint to look like stone and wood. Give a final coat of diluted PVA for extra strength. The castle will fold flat to store.

5

HOW TO MAKE A POCKET SIEGE ENGINE

Before the invention of gunpowder, fearsome machines called trebuchets were used to attack castles. Anything from huge rocks, dead horses and even the occasional foreign ambassador could be flung over the castle walls.

YOU'LL NEED:

2 oblong plastic ice-cream tub lids (1-litre size), sticky tape, double-sided tape, scissors, ruler, fine marker pen, some not very important homework for ammunition.

A FARMER IN ENGLAND HAS BUILT HIS OWN FULL-SIZE MEDIEVAL SIEGE ENGINE. IT CAN FLING A PIANO 125 METRES. IN TEXAS, THEY ARE WORKING ON A MODEL FOR THROWING '57 BUICKS.

1 Eat all the ice-cream.

2 Cut a rectangle 8 x 14 cm from lid 1. Keep the rest.

3 Mark and score four lines. (See the inside front cover for how to do the scoring.)

4 Cut a 2-cm slot at A.

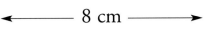
← 8 cm →

| Tab A | Double-sided tape |

2 cm

2.5 cm

5 cm

Slot A
2 cm

2.5 cm

| Tab B | Double-sided tape |

2 cm

5 Fold along the scored lines. Stick tab A and tab B to lid 2 with double-sided tape.

6 Cut a length 15 x 1 cm from the edge of lid 1.

Scrunched-up paper

8 Cut a short length from the edge of lid 1 for an ammo holder. Stick to the other end with tape.

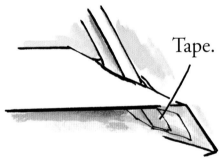
Tape.

7 Push one end through slot A and secure with double-sided tape.

9 Press down, load ammo and fire.

HOW TO MAKE A MAYPOLE

May Day was a very important festival in the Middle Ages. It celebrated the end of winter and the flowering of spring. In many countries in Europe there was feasting and games and dancing round the maypole. A May queen was chosen and crowned with a garland of wild flowers.

YOU'LL NEED:
1 x 1-litre screw-top drink carton, 10-cm round plastic lid, strong paper 45 x 12 cm, 7 different-coloured ribbons 40 cm long, scissors, coloured sticky tape, ruler, glue, pencil, scraps of green material.

TOP TIP - TOP TIP
Cut out some small paper flowers and stick them to the Maypole.

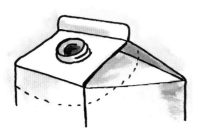

1 Remove the cap and open up the top of the carton.

2 Cut round the screw-top in a circle.

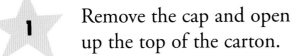

3 Glue it to the plastic lid.

4 Knot the ribbons together and glue to the corner of the paper.

5 Roll up the paper and trim the end.

6 Adjust the width and height of the paper tube by pulling it gently. Glue the end inside the screw-top.

7 Use coloured sticky tape to strengthen and decorate your maypole.

8 Glue scraps of green material over the base.

HOW TO SAY IT WITH FLOWERS

People have always loved flowers and each one has its own meaning. In the Middle Ages a knight could give his sweetheart certain flowers to show his love for her. She could then reply appropriately. It was very handy if you were shy or just wanted to say 'get lost'!

YOU'LL NEED:
Paper, small piece of card, pencil, tracing paper, masking tape, scissors, glue, compass, wire bag ties, paints and brushes.

TOP TIP - TOP TIP
Cut out several petals at a time by drawing on folded paper.

1 Copy the templates on to the card (see the instructions on the inside front cover). Cut them out.

Petal

Centre

 **2** Draw round the templates on to the paper to make five petals and one centre. Cut them out.

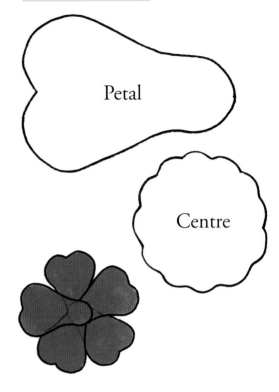

3 Paint the petals red on both sides. Paint the centre gold.

4 Arrange the petals one over the other like this and glue together.

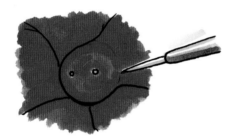

5 Make two holes with the compass through the middle.

6 Thread through the bag tie and twist it together.

Red rose
True love
Pink rose
secret
love

7 Glue on the gold centre.

Find out the meanings of some more flowers.

11

MAP OF EUROPE

in the Middle Ages

1066

The Battle of Hastings. The Normans conquer England.

1215

King John of England signs the Magna Carta promising that laws will be good and fair.

1300

First use of cannons and gunpowder in Europe.

1347-49
The Black Death wipes out a third of Europe's population.

1447
Printing with moveable type invented in Germany.

1492
Columbus discovers America.

HOW TO MAKE A MEDIEVAL PUDDING

Choosing what to have for pudding was a different matter in the olden days. It wasn't as easy as looking in the freezer. Fruits, especially soft berries, were difficult to store and had to be freshly picked when they were in season.

KITCHENWARE YOU'LL NEED:

Small jug, large ovenproof dish, food processor, large bowl, 2 tablespoons, small pan or microwave.

INGREDIENTS YOU'LL NEED:

1 x 500-g bag frozen summer fruits, 1 x 340-g tub frozen raspberries (all defrosted), about 4 tablespoons clear honey, 125 g multigrain bread, 100 g chopped hazelnuts (optional) but, if not using, add 100 g more bread.

Yes we have no chocolate, potatoes or tomatoes, but I've made a lovely fruit crumble!

MUCH OF OUR FAVOURITE FOOD WAS UNKNOWN IN EUROPE UNTIL COLUMBUS DISCOVERED AMERICA IN 1492. THANKS CHRIS.

★ 1 Wash your hands. Open the packets of fruit and pour the juice into the small jug.

★ 2 Put the fruit into the ovenproof dish. Drizzle about 3 heaped tablespoons of honey over it.

★ 3 Remove the crusts and break the bread into chunks. Chop in the food processor to make large breadcrumbs.

★ 4 Put them into the large bowl and add the nuts (if using). Mix together.

★ 5 Spread them over the fruit. Bake in a moderate oven for 20-25 minutes.

★ 6 Gently heat the juice. Add about 1 heaped tablespoon of honey and serve with the pudding.

HOW TO PLAY THREE MEN'S MERELS

Merels is one of the oldest games in the world still played today. It was very popular in the Middle Ages. Merel boards have been found carved in the stones of Europe's great cathedrals. There are several versions. Three men's merels is the simplest. It's really good. Learn to play this using the board on the opposite page, then you can try the harder one, nine men's merels.

YOU'LL NEED:
2 sets of 3 counters and someone to play with.

TOP TIP - TOP TIP
Coloured bottle tops make really good counters.

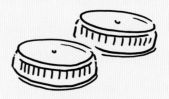

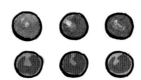

flip

1 Decide who goes first. Each player has three counters.

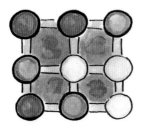

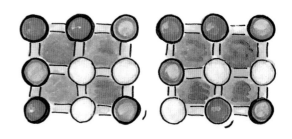

2 Take turns to place a counter on a blank spot until all six are used up.

3 Move one of your counters to a free spot next to it.

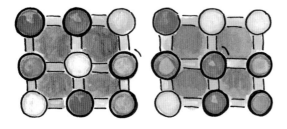

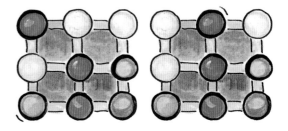

4 The aim is to get your three counters in a row called a mill. They can go across, up or down, but not diagonally.

5 You have won when you get a mill or the other player cannot move.

HOW TO DRAW AN ILLUMINATED LETTER

Before the invention of printing, every book was written and drawn by hand. Some books took years to finish and were so valuable that they had to be chained up. Each page began with a large beautifully decorated capital letter.

I'm just dotting the **i**s, crossing the **t**s and adding a large sea serpent to each **S**. I'll be about two years.

YOU'LL NEED:

Paper, graph paper, pencil, ruler, compass, black, coloured and metallic pens, paints and brushes, scissors, glue.

TOP TIP - TOP TIP

Try writing your initials like this.

1 Draw a big outline of your letter in pencil on graph paper. Use the ruler and compass.

2 Add flowers or animals or funny faces.

3 Paint in the colours and allow to dry. If you like, use your metallic pens too.

4 Go over the outlines in black pen. Cut out the square and stick to your paper to continue your writing.

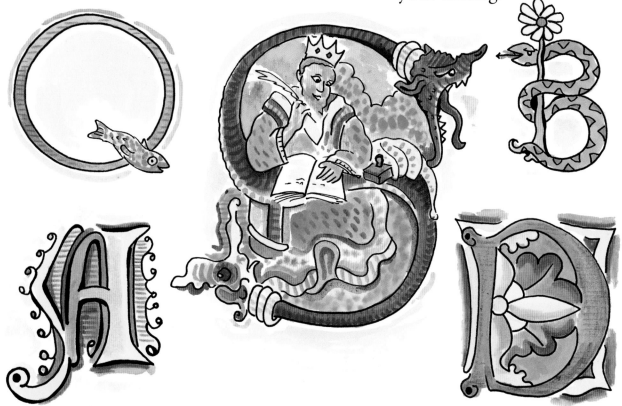

HOW TO MAKE A COAT OF ARMS

Coats of arms were invented in the Middle Ages. Each knight had their own special design. They were the medieval equivalent of today's logos and brand names. Use your stencils and the examples on the following pages to make your own. Look up your name on the internet, your family may have one already.

YOU'LL NEED:
Paper or thin card, pencil, coloured pens, paints and brushes, ruler, stencils.

HERALDIC PAINT BOX
These were the colours used in coats of arms. They had to be bright and easy to see in battle.

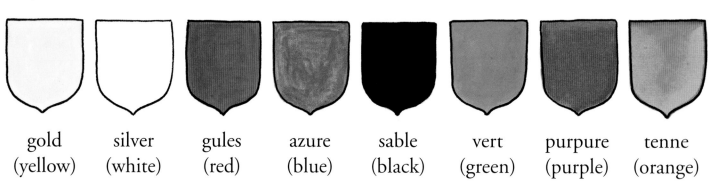

| gold (yellow) | silver (white) | gules (red) | azure (blue) | sable (black) | vert (green) | purpure (purple) | tenne (orange) |

sword

dragon

lion

heart

star

lozenge

cross

roundel

crescent

bell

fleur-de-lis

shield

sheaf

conch shell

shamrock

sun

castle

crown

HOW TO CREATE AN HERALDIC MONSTER

The knights used pictures of fierce animals like lions, leopards and dragons on their shields. They also made up animals. A Gryphon had the head and wings of an eagle and the body of a lion. Why not make up your own? Here are two examples.

Guineafish

Caterigar

Unicorn

Salamander

Gryphon

Copy the shield template on to paper
or card (see the instructions on the inside
front cover). Use the stencils to design your
own coat of arms. Then try creating a logo
with simple pictures of your favourite
things: perhaps a dolphin, a mobile
phone or a huge chocolate
cake with cherries
on top.

TEMPLATE

HOW TO USE YOUR STENCILS

Cut or tear off the stencil sheet from the back of the book. Choose a shape and place it over your paper. Hold it in place with masking tape. Draw the outline with pencil or pen. Use pages 20-23 as a guide to colouring and adding detail to your shapes.

YE OLDE PAINT DABBER

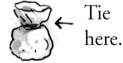
← Tie here.

1 You'll need a piece of cloth about 10 cm square – bandage is good – made into a pad.

TOP TIPS – TOP TIPS
★ Practise on scrap paper first!
★ Make sure the paint isn't too runny.
★ You can use this technique to make backgrounds.

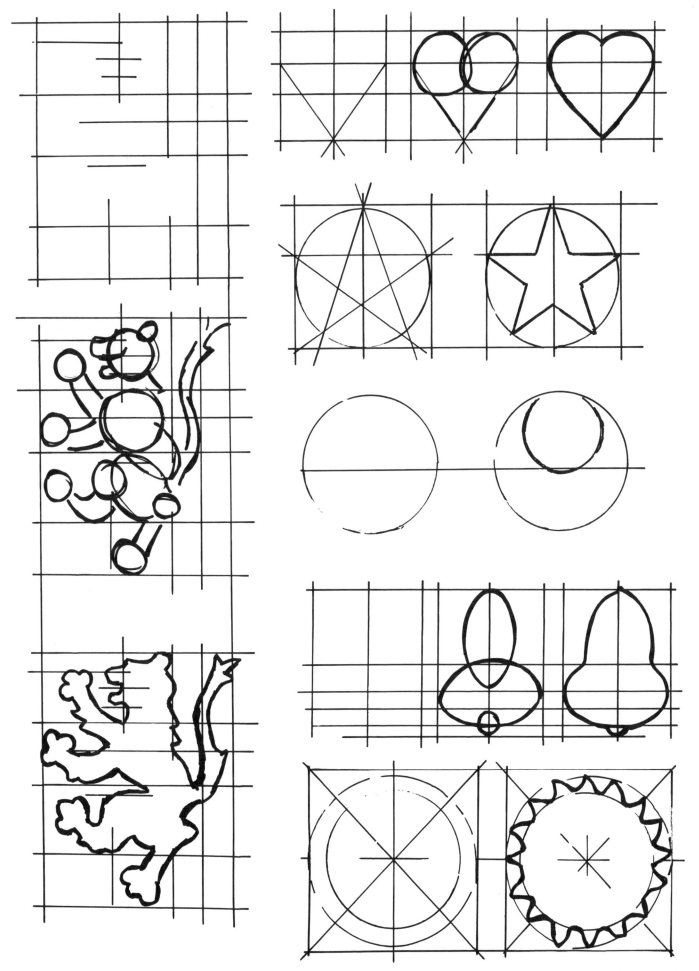

XXV

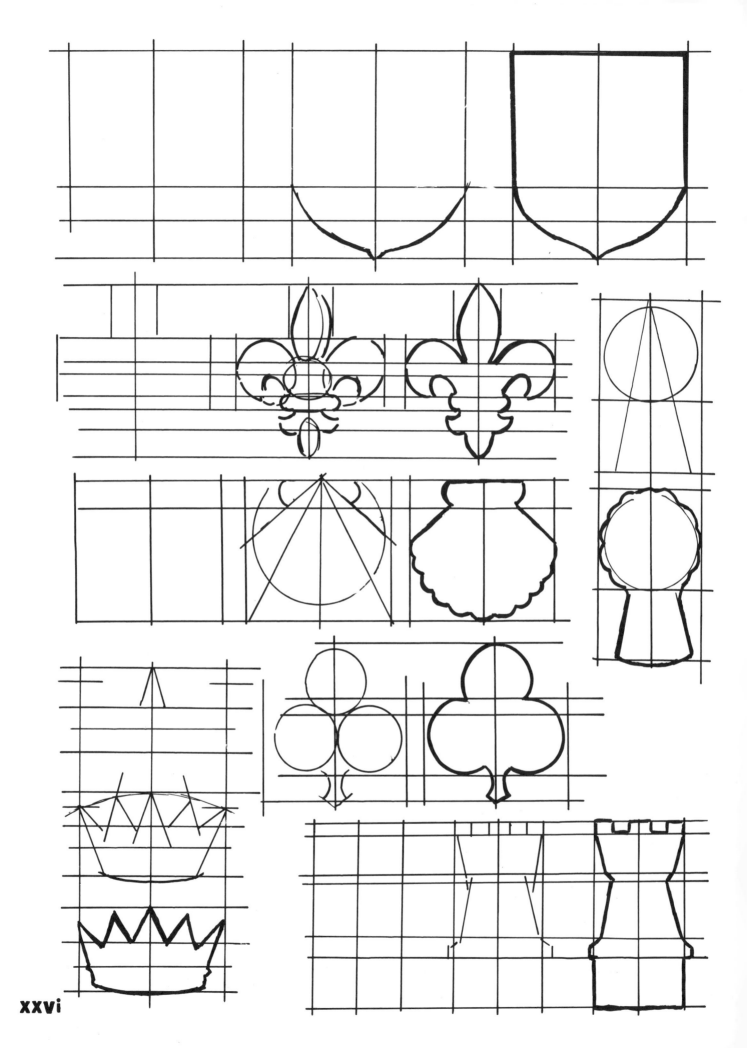